DANGER
DANGER
HOT
HOT
SAUCE!

DANGER
DANGER
HOT
HOT
SAUCE!

TRY THESE RECIPES
IF YOU DARE!

This edition published by Parragon Books Ltd in 2014
LOVE FOOD is an imprint of Parragon Books Ltd

Parragon Books Ltd
Chartist House
15–17 Trim Street
Bath BA1 1HA, UK
www.parragon.com/lovefood

Copyright © Parragon Books Ltd 2014

LOVE FOOD and the accompanying heart device is a registered trademark of Parragon Books Ltd in Australia, the UK, USA, India and the EU.

ISBN 978-1-4723-2984-4

Printed in China

New recipes written by Beverly Le Blanc
Introduction and incidental text by Dominic Utton and Beverly Le Blanc
New photography by Mike Cooper
New home economy by Lincoln Jefferson
Additional design work by Sîan Williams
Internal illustrations by Julie Ingham and Nicola O'Byrne

Notes for the Reader
This book uses both metric and imperial measurements. Follow the same units of measurement throughout; do not mix metric and imperial. All spoon measurements are level: teaspoons are assumed to be 5 ml, and tablespoons are assumed to be 15 ml. Unless otherwise stated, milk is assumed to be full fat, eggs and individual vegetables are medium, and pepper is freshly ground black pepper. Unless otherwise stated, all root vegetables should be peeled prior to using.

Garnishes, decorations and serving suggestions are all optional and not necessarily included in the recipe ingredients or method. The times given are an approximate guide only. Preparation times differ according to the techniques used by different people and the cooking times may also vary from those given. Optional ingredients, variations or serving suggestions have not been included in the time calculations.

Picture acknowledgements
The publisher would like to thank the following for permission to reproduce copyright material: Cover illustrations courtesy of iStock; page 7: Christopher Columbus © De Agostini Picture Library/De Agostini /A. Dagli Orti; page 103: Chilli pepper on windowsill © Dorling Kindersley/Peter Anderson.

CONTENTS

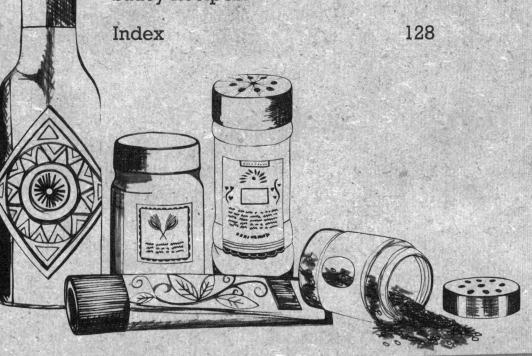

THE HISTORY OF CHILLIES

Everyone knows the rhyme: in 1492 Columbus sailed the ocean blue….Well, lovers of spicy food can add another line – he also found the chilli too! Before the discovery of the New World, the chilli was a secret kept only by the South and Central Americans, where it had been used in their diet since 7500 BCE.

Columbus 'discovered' the chilli in the Caribbean and thought it simply another variety of pepper. But although varieties were duly shipped back to Europe, the plants were viewed mostly as curiosities, with their heat occasionally being used for medicinal purposes.

Traders heading elsewhere from the Americas, however, found a different, far more welcoming market. Chillies were brought to West Africa, where they immediately became a naturalized plant. And South Asia especially embraced the fiery flavours, incorporating chillies into their cuisine, perhaps because they were already familiar with pungent, spicy dishes but also because the plants were cheap to grow, meaning it was as

likely to be eaten by the common labourers as the aristocracy.

Gradually the chilli spread across all Asia – and with the wonderful flavours came a host of superstitious beliefs about the properties of the potent little plant. It was believed they had the power to ward off the evil eye and most households would have a bunch of chillies hanging over the threshold to deter evil spirits. A handful of chillies mixed with ash from the hearth would also be waved over a man's head for good luck or to protect him from bad magic.

Although it took chillies just 50 years to spread from South America across the whole world, Europeans took longer to appreciate the taste. Spanish and Portuguese monks had started cooking with them during the mid-16th century, but the little vegetable with the big kick

remained a niche taste for much of the continent until the 20th century.

So the next time somebody tells you chillies come from India, be sure to correct them – it took a European explorer to bring chillies to Asia in the first place!

THE HOT SAUCE BASICS

There's more to making a good hot sauce than just chopping up a couple of chillies. But with a bit of judicious selection, common storecupboard ingredients can produce an astonishing variety of flavours and add complexity to your sauces. Try using the ingredients below then experiment with quantities and varieties to make a customized version.

HERBS AND SPICES
Whether fresh or dried, these provide a depth of flavour. Jamaican Jerk Sizzling Sauce, for example, wouldn't taste authentic without dried allspice, and Chimichurri Sweltering Sauce relies on a medley of fresh herbs.

CHILLIES
The essential ingredient in most hot sauce recipes, these come in a wide range of varieties and heats.

OIL
Essential for frying chillies and other ingredients and for adding body to sauces. Keep a selection – sunflower, rapeseed, groundnut, olive – to ring the flavour changes.

SALT
Always essential to bring out individual flavours.

SUGAR
White and brown sugars provide a counterpoint to hot spiciness and act as a preservative. Always dissolve sugar before bringing a sauce to the boil to prevent crystals forming.

VINEGAR
Caribbean and many traditional North American sauces contain distilled white vinegar, but cider or red and white wine vinegars are also good. They provide a sour background, as well as acting as a preservative.

HOW TO HANDLE CHILLIES

It is the capsaicin in a chilli that provides the heat and, as a rule, the smaller and thinner a chilli is the hotter it will taste (because it proportionally contains more seeds). All of a chilli's capsaicin is produced in a gland running down the middle of the fruit and the seeds clustered around this bit are the hottest part.

Be careful when you are chopping chillies, especially if you are removing the gland or the seeds. If your skin is sensitive, wear plastic gloves and never touch your eyes or mouth after handling chillies without thoroughly washing your hands first. You can also protect your hands by rubbing them first with vegetable oil, which acts as a barrier.

Pan-frying chillies can also release a potent vapour that may irritate your eyes, so set the extractor to high before starting or open a window. This is especially important when using the hot, hot, hot chillies in the Blow Your Head Off chapter!

Warning! The next time your mouth feels like it is on fire, don't drink a glass of water – that only spreads the heat around. Reach instead for milk or yogurt: dairy ingredients help to dilute the heat more effectively than anything else. It's not by chance that in India, for example, yogurt raita is always served with hot curries!

STORING HOT SAUCES

Although some sauces, such as Searing Serrano & Coriander, are best made just before serving and eaten immediately, others made with fresh ingredients, such as Creole Gumbo Flamin' Sauce, will keep for up to two days in the fridge in an airtight container. Those with lots of vinegar or sugar, such as Louisiana Hot Pepper Sauce, can be kept even longer – up to a month when sealed in the refrigerator. For longer storage, some sauces can be frozen or placed in sterilized jars. But don't worry! Each recipe in this book includes specific instructions for storage.

FREEZING SAUCES

Always freeze sauces in small containers so you never defrost more than you need. After making the sauce, let it cool to room temperature, then pour it into freezerproof containers, leaving a 1-cm/½-inch space at the top. Cover and label with the date. Most freezer-friendly sauces will freeze for up to a year, but they are best eaten within 3 months before the flavours dull. Thaw at room temperature when ready to serve.

STERILIZING JARS

1. Only use jars intended for preserving and never use jars with cracks or chips. Wash the jars and lids in hot, soapy water and rinse. If the recipe contains vinegar, use an acid-proof lid.

2. Place the jars upright in a heavy-based saucepan that is 5 cm/2 inches deeper than the jars. Pour over enough boiling water to submerge the jars and boil for 15 minutes.

3. Use tongs to carefully remove the jars and leave them to drain on clean tea towels.

FILLING JARS FOR SHORT-TERM STORAGE

1. Use a funnel to pour the hot sauce into the hot jars. Leave a space of 1 cm/½ inch between the sauce and the top of the jar. Wipe the rim, then secure the lid.

2. Leave the sauce to cool, then store at room temperature for up to a month, and refrigerate once opened. The length of time the sauce will last in the fridge depends on the vinegar and sugar content, so please see the storage information on the recipes for how long the sauce will last in the refrigerator.

USING A WATER BATH FOR LONGER STORAGE

1. For longer storage, use specific preserving jars, that have a two-part lid with a screw band, and fill as above. Position a rack in the bottom of a deep saucepan or use a preserving pan. Arrange the filled jars upright on the rack or in the pan.

2. Pour over enough boiling water to fully submerge the jars, return the water to the boil and boil for 20 minutes for a 300-ml/10-fl oz jar or 30 minutes for a 600-ml/1-pint jar.

3. Use tongs to remove the jars. Leave to cool to room temperature. If kept sealed, the jars will store for a year. Once opened, keep refrigerated and use for the amount of time stated in the recipe.

WARMING UP!

FEEL THE HEAT WITH THE SCOVILLE SCALE!

How do you measure the heat of a chilli? With science, as it turns out!

In 1912, the American pharmacist Wilbur Scoville devised the Scoville Organoleptic Test (now simply called the Scoville Scale) to measure the piquancy, or hotness, of chilli peppers. The heat of a chilli comes from capsaicin and the Scoville Scale measures how much capsaicin is present in any given chilli.

Although technology has moved on in the 100 years since Scoville devised his method, his principles remain – and chillies are still measured according to his scale.

SCOVILLE HEAT UNITS	CHILLI EXAMPLES
1,500,000-2,100,000	Trinidad Moruga Scorpion (the hottest known chilli in the world!)
855,000-1,463,700	Naga Viper, Infinity, Bhut Jolokia
350,000-855,000	Red Savina Habanero, Indian Tezpur
100,000-350,000	Habanero, Scotch Bonnet, Datil
50,000-100,000	Santaka, Chiltecpin, Peri Peri, Bird's Eye Chilli
30,000-50,000	Cayenne, Tabasco, Pequin, Aji
15,000-30,000	Chile de Arbol
5,000-15,000	Yellow Wax, Serrano
2,500-5,000	Jalapeño, Mirasol, Chipotle, Poblano
1,500-2,500	Sandia, Cascabel
1,000-1,500	Pasilla, Anaheim, Ancho, Española
100-1,000	Pimento, Pepperoncini

KETCHUP WITH A KICK

This is a great recipe for the time when tomatoes are at their cheapest and most plentiful. Make up large batches of this ketchup, following the storage instructions on page 10, and enjoy the taste of summer all year round.

MAKES: ABOUT 600 ML/ 1 PINT **PREP TIME: 15 MINS** **COOK TIME: 2¼ HRS**

INGREDIENTS
2.25 kg/5 lb ripe, juicy tomatoes, roughly chopped

2 red jalapeño chillies, roughly chopped

1 sweet white onion, roughly chopped

1 tsp salt, plus extra to taste

1 tsp fennel seeds

1 tsp black mustard seeds

250 ml/9 fl oz cider vinegar or white wine vinegar

100 g/3½ oz soft light brown sugar

1 cinnamon stick

½ tsp ground nutmeg

½ tsp sweet paprika

1–3 tsp cayenne pepper, to taste

1–2 tbsp tomato purée (optional)

pepper

1. Put the tomatoes, chillies, onion and salt into a large saucepan over a high heat. Stir until the tomatoes begin to break down, then reduce the heat to low, cover and simmer for 30 minutes, or until the tomatoes are pulpy.

2. Meanwhile, put the fennel seeds and mustard seeds on a square of muslin, bring together the sides and tie to make a bag, then set aside.

3. Pass the tomato mixture through a sieve into a large saucepan, rubbing backwards and forwards with a wooden spoon and scraping the base of the sieve to produce as much purée as possible.

4. Add the spice bag and the vinegar, sugar, cinnamon stick, nutmeg, paprika and cayenne pepper. Season to taste with pepper, then stir until the sugar dissolves. Bring to the boil, then reduce the heat and simmer, uncovered, for 1½ hours, skimming the surface as necessary, until the sauce is reduced and thickened. Transfer to a bowl and leave to cool.

5. Depending on how well-flavoured the tomatoes were you might want to add some tomato purée. Remove the spice bag and cinnamon stick.

6. Leave the ketchup to cool completely. It can be used immediately, or stored in an airtight container in the refrigerator for up to 1 month. For guidelines on longer storage, see page 10. This sauce can also be frozen for up to 3 months, see page 10.

BLAZING BARBECUE SAUCE

This is the perfect sauce to spice up any barbecue and tastes great when served with burgers, meat skewers or chicken wings, fresh from the barbecue grill.

MAKES: ABOUT 225 ML/ 8 FL OZ **PREP TIME: 5 MINS** **COOK TIME: 20 MINS**

INGREDIENTS

1 tbsp olive oil
1 small onion, finely chopped
2–3 garlic cloves, crushed
1 red jalapeño chilli, finely chopped
2 tsp tomato purée
1 tsp (or to taste) dry mustard
1 tbsp red wine vinegar
1 tbsp Worcestershire sauce
2–3 tsp muscovado sugar
300 ml/10 fl oz water

1. Heat the oil in a small heavy-based saucepan, add the onion, garlic and chilli, and gently sauté, stirring frequently, for 3 minutes, or until beginning to soften. Remove from the heat.

2. Blend the tomato purée with the mustard, the vinegar and the Worcestershire sauce to a paste, then stir into the onion mixture with 2 teaspoons of the sugar. Mix well, then gradually stir in the water. Add more sugar, if desired.

3. Return to the heat and bring to the boil, stirring frequently. Reduce the heat and gently simmer, stirring occasionally, for 15 minutes. Remove from the heat and leave to cool completely. The sauce can be used immediately, or stored in an airtight container in the refrigerator for up to 2 weeks. For guidelines on longer storage, see page 10.

SWELTERING SWEET CHILLI SAUCE

It can be tempting to reach for a ready-made jar of this dipping sauce when serving crisp Chinese egg rolls or wontons, but this is so easy to make there isn't any reason to waste money on the commercial variety!

MAKES: ABOUT 150 ML/ 5 FL OZ   **PREP TIME: 5 MINS**   **COOK TIME: 25 MINS**

INGREDIENTS

4 red jalapeño chillies, halved

2 large garlic cloves, roughly chopped

4-cm/1½-inch piece fresh ginger, roughly chopped

150 ml/5 fl oz rice wine or cider vinegar

150 g/5½ oz caster sugar

150 ml/5 fl oz water

2 tbsp dried chilli flakes

¼ tsp salt

1. Put the chillies, garlic and ginger into a small food processor and pulse until finely chopped but not puréed, scraping down the side as necessary. Alternatively, finely chop the chillies, garlic and ginger with a sharp knife.

2. Add the vinegar, sugar, water and blend together.

3. Transfer the ingredients to a heavy-based saucepan over a high heat. Add the chilli flakes and salt, stirring to dissolve the sugar.

4. Bring to the boil, without stirring. Reduce the heat to medium–low and simmer, stirring frequently so the sauce doesn't stick to the base of the pan, for about 20 minutes, or until thickened.

5. Transfer the sauce to a bowl and leave to cool completely, stirring occasionally. The sauce can be used immediately, or stored in an airtight container in the refrigerator for up to 2 weeks. For guidelines on longer storage, see page 10.

PIQUANT PICO DE GALLO SAUCE

Hot and fresh flavours mingle in this simple Mexican salsa-like sauce, which adds a burst of chilli heat to everything from a bowl of tortilla chips to grilled meat and tacos.

MAKES: ABOUT 175 ML/ 6 FL OZ

PREP TIME: 10 MINS

COOK TIME: NONE

INGREDIENTS

150 ml/5 fl oz passata

2 tbsp freshly squeezed lime juice or orange juice, or to taste

2 large pickled garlic cloves or fresh garlic cloves, very finely chopped

½ sweet white onion, finely chopped

2 tbsp pickled jalapeño chillies, drained and finely chopped

½ tsp ancho chilli powder

small handful of coriander leaves, finely chopped, to garnish

salt and pepper

1. Combine the passata and lime juice in a non-metallic bowl and season to taste with salt and pepper. Add all the remaining ingredients, except the coriander leaves.

2. The sauce can be served immediately, but will benefit from being left to stand at room temperature for 30 minutes for the flavours to blend. Stir well before serving and adjust the lime juice and salt and pepper, if necessary. Sprinkle with coriander just before serving.

3. If there is any sauce left over, pour over a layer of olive oil, cover and store in the refrigerator for up to 3 days. Stir in the oil just before serving and garnish with chopped fresh coriander.

HERO TIPS

Still not hot enough? Use red or green Thai chillies instead of the jalapeños, or add ½ tsp Louisiana Hot Pepper Sauce (see page 80) for a real blast of heat.

ROASTING ROADHOUSE STEAK SAUCE

Savoury and sweet with a blast of heat from the cayenne pepper, this rich sauce complements any steak it is paired with. It also makes a great marinade for pork chops.

MAKES: ABOUT 350 ML/ 12 FL OZ

PREP TIME: 10 MINS

COOK TIME: 50 MINS

INGREDIENTS

400 g/14 oz canned chopped tomatoes

150 ml/5 fl oz beef stock

4 garlic cloves, chopped

1 red onion, finely chopped

175 g/6 oz raisins

4 tbsp Worcestershire sauce

1 tbsp beef extract or rich beef stock cube, crumbled

1 tbsp mustard powder, dissolved in 1 tbsp water

2 tbsp white wine vinegar

1 tbsp golden syrup

1 tbsp soft dark brown sugar

½ tsp cayenne pepper

finely grated zest of 1 orange

salt and pepper

1. Mix together all the ingredients with salt and pepper to taste in a heavy-based saucepan over a high heat, stirring to dissolve the golden syrup and sugar. Bring to the boil, then reduce the heat to very low and simmer, stirring freqently, for 30 minutes, or until the mixture is blended and the raisins are falling apart.

2. Transfer the mixture to a blender or food processor and purée. Strain the mixture through a fine sieve into the cleaned pan, rubbing backwards and forwards with a wooden spoon and scraping the base of the sieve to produce as much purée as possible.

3. Place the pan over a medium heat and bring the purée to the boil. Reduce the heat to medium–low and simmer, uncovered, for 15 minutes, or until the sauce has thickened and reduced. Transfer to a bowl and leave to cool completely. Adjust the salt and pepper to taste.

4. The sauce can be used immediately, or stored in an airtight container in the refrigerator for up to 3 weeks. For guidelines on longer storage, see page 10.

SWELTERING SATAY SAUCE

The traditionally mild peanut sauce is heated up in this version with the addition of Indonesian chilli paste (sambal oelek). It's sold in most Asian food shops but the intensity of the heat varies with the brand.

MAKES: ABOUT 175 ML/ 6 FL OZ **PREP TIME: 10 MINS** **COOK TIME: 5 MINS**

INGREDIENTS

- 2 tbsp sunflower oil
- 2 shallots, finely chopped
- 1 large garlic clove, finely chopped
- 2.5-cm/1-inch piece fresh ginger, finely chopped
- 1–3 tsp Indonesian chilli paste (sambal oelek)
- 100 g/3½ oz creamed coconut, dissolved in 250 ml/9 fl oz boiling water
- 5 tbsp crunchy peanut butter
- 1 tsp tamarind paste or freshly squeezed lime juice, or to taste
- 1 tsp dark soy sauce, or to taste
- 4 tbsp water, if needed
- 4 red jalapeño chillies, deseeded and thinly sliced
- salt and pepper

1. Heat the oil in a wok over a high heat until very hot. Add the shallots, garlic and ginger and stir-fry for 1–2 minutes, or until the shallots are soft and just beginning to colour. Stir in the chilli paste, to taste, and continue frying for a further 30 seconds.

2. Add the creamed coconut and peanut butter, stirring until blended. Stir in the tamarind paste and soy sauce, season to taste with pepper and continue stirring over a medium heat for 2–3 minutes. If the mixture looks separated, stir in the water and beat well. Stir in the chillies. Adjust the seasoning, if necessary, and add extra chilli paste, tamarind paste and soy sauce, to taste.

3. The sauce can be served hot or at room temperature, or left to cool completely and stored in an airtight container in the refrigerator for up to 1 week.

HERO TIPS

If using an unfamiliar brand of sambal oelek, start with the lesser amount and add the remaining chilli paste at the end if the sauce isn't hot enough.

FIERY ROASTED TOMATO SAUCE

This sauce, with its paprika and sherry ingredients, has a Spanish flavour and is great when served as a dip with tortilla chips or as an accompaniment to Spanish omelette and chips.

MAKES: ABOUT 175 ML/ 6 FL OZ   **PREP TIME: 10 MINS**   **COOK TIME: 45 MINS**

INGREDIENTS
6 vine-ripened tomatoes

1 red pepper, cut into quarters and deseeded

1 garlic clove, unpeeled

1 red onion, cut into quarters

4 tbsp olive oil

1 small red jalapeño chilli, very finely chopped

1 tsp hot paprika

1 tbsp sherry

salt and pepper

1. Preheat the oven to 180°C/350°F/Gas Mark 4.

2. Lay out the vegetables on a large baking tray, brush with olive oil, then roast in the oven, turning once halfway through cooking, for about 45 minutes or until they are blistered and slightly charred.

3. Leave to cool. When cool enough to handle, peel the tomatoes and red pepper, and squeeze the garlic from its skin. Transfer the tomato, red pepper, garlic flesh and onion to a food processor and process to a fairly smooth consistency.

4. Spoon the mixture into a large serving bowl and stir in the chilli, paprika and sherry. Season to taste. The sauce can be used immediately or left to cool completely and stored in an airtight container in the refrigerator for up to 1 week.

HERO TIPS

The tablespoon of sherry in this recipe can also be replaced by Madeira, which is a fortified wine from Portugal.

CREAMY BUT DEADLY MUSTARD SAUCE

The pale colour of this sauce belies its hot flavour; this comes from the mustard powder with extra heat from the cayenne pepper – the heat kicks in at the back of the mouth and lingers after swallowing.

MAKES: ABOUT 225 ML/ 8 FL OZ   **PREP TIME: 5 MINS**   **COOK TIME: 25 MINS**

INGREDIENTS

1 tbsp olive oil

4 shallots, thinly sliced

1 large garlic clove, very finely chopped

2 tbsp mustard powder

2 tsp cayenne pepper

300 ml/10 fl oz beef stock, chicken stock or vegetable stock

150 ml/5 fl oz crème fraîche or soured cream

1 tbsp wholegrain mustard

freshly squeezed lemon juice, to taste (optional)

salt and pepper

1. Heat the oil in a lidded frying pan over a medium heat. Add the shallots, cover with a piece of crumpled, wet greaseproof paper, then cover the pan. Reduce the heat to very low and leave the shallots to cook for 5–8 minutes, or until soft.

2. Uncover, remove the paper and increase the heat. Add the garlic and stir for 1 minute. Stir in the mustard powder and cayenne pepper.

3. Slowly whisk in the stock, whisking constantly so the mustard doesn't form lumps. Bring to the boil and boil for 5–8 minutes, stirring constantly, until reduced by half.

4. Stir in the crème fraîche and return to the boil. Reduce the heat and simmer for 10 minutes, or until reduced to a coating consistency. Stir in the wholegrain mustard and season to taste with salt and pepper. Add 1–2 teaspoons of lemon juice, if using, to cut through the richness.

5. The sauce can be served immediately, or left to cool completely and stored in an airtight container in the refrigerator for up to 2 days. Reheat to serve.

HOT-AS-HELL HORSERADISH SAUCE

This quick and easy sauce gets its punchy heat from freshly grated horseradish. It's traditionally added to seafood cocktails but a spoonful or two can be stirred into home-made tomato soup for an extra kick.

MAKES: ABOUT 150 ML/ 5 FL OZ　　　　**PREP TIME: 10 MINS**　　　　**COOK TIME: NONE**

INGREDIENTS

125 g/4½ oz tomato ketchup, plus extra, if necessary

2.5-cm/1-inch piece horseradish, finely grated, or 1 tbsp grated horseradish

1 tbsp freshly squeezed lemon juice, or to taste, plus extra, if needed

pepper

1. Put the ketchup and horseradish into a bowl and stir to combine.

2. Add the lemon juice, and pepper to taste. Stir to combine, then add extra lemon juice, to taste.

3. The sauce can be served immediately, or stored in an airtight container in the refrigerator for up to 3 weeks. After 1–2 days the sauce will thicken, so you will need to beat in extra ketchup or lemon juice with a fork when ready to serve.

INTENSE ITALIAN ARRABBIATA SAUCE

Arrabbiata sauce is a classic Italian sauce and translates as 'angry' in Italian, due to the fiery nature of the chillies! It is usually served as an accompaniment to pasta.

MAKES: ABOUT 600 ML/ 1 PINT

PREP TIME: 10 MINS

COOK TIME: 20 MINS

INGREDIENTS

2 tbsp olive oil

2 garlic cloves, chopped

1 red serrano chilli, deseeded and chopped

1 tbsp grated lemon rind

450 g/1 lb ripe tomatoes, peeled and chopped

1 tbsp tomato purée, blended with 150 ml/5 fl oz water

pinch of caster sugar

1 tbsp balsamic vinegar

1 tbsp chopped fresh marjoram

pepper

1. Heat the oil in a heavy-based saucepan over a medium heat, add the garlic and chilli and sauté, stirring constantly, for 1 minute.

2. Sprinkle in the lemon rind and stir, then add the tomatoes with the blended tomato purée. Add the sugar and bring to the boil, then reduce the heat and simmer for 12 minutes. Add pepper to taste.

3. Add the vinegar and marjoram and simmer for a further 5 minutes. The sauce can be used immediately or left to cool completely and stored in an airtight container in the refrigerator for up to 1 week.

HERO TIPS

This sauce is best served with freshly cooked penne pasta. Spoon the sauce over the pasta and then sprinkle with parsley and Parmesan cheese.

KICKIN' CON CARNE SAUCE

Chilli con carne sauce is a perennial favourite and the combination here of smoky ancho chilli powder and hot, hot, hot cayenne pepper gives this version a great kick!

MAKES: ABOUT 600 ML/ 1 PINT   **PREP TIME: 10 MINS**   **COOK TIME: 20 MINS**

INGREDIENTS

2 tbsp sunflower oil

1 onion, finely chopped

1 red pepper, deseeded and chopped

2 large garlic cloves, chopped

2 tsp ancho chilli powder

2 tsp ground coriander

2 tsp ground cumin

1½ tsp cayenne pepper, or to taste

400 g/14 oz canned chopped tomatoes

350 ml/12 fl oz passata

1 tbsp dried thyme, marjoram or Mexican oregano

½ tsp sugar

salt and pepper

1. Heat the oil in a large frying pan over a medium–high heat. Add the onion and red pepper and fry, stirring, for 3–5 minutes, or until soft. Add the garlic, chilli powder, coriander, cumin and cayenne pepper and stir for a further minute.

2. Add the tomatoes, passata, thyme and sugar and season with salt and pepper. Bring to the boil, stirring, then reduce the heat so the liquid just bubbles and leave to cook for 15–20 minutes until the sauce reduces by about half.

3. Transfer the sauce to a food processor or blender and purée.

4. The sauce can be used immediately, or left to cool completely and stored in an airtight container in the refrigerator for up to 3 days. This sauce can be frozen for up to 3 months, see page 10.

HERO TIPS

Double the quantities and have several portions of this in the freezer ready to make chilli con carne to warm up winter evenings.

BLISTERING BEER & CHILLI SAUCE

Fire up the heat of any barbecue with this sauce packed with chilli flavour. Definitely a barbecue sauce for adults, with pale ale, treacle and heat from cayenne pepper, ancho chilli powder and fresh jalapeño chillies replacing the sickly sweetness of so many barbecue sauces.

MAKES: ABOUT 450 ML/ 16 FL OZ   **PREP TIME: 10 MINS**   **COOK TIME: 45 MINS**

INGREDIENTS
2 tbsp sunflower oil
1 red onion, finely chopped
1 tbsp ancho chilli powder
1½ tsp cayenne pepper
250 g/9 oz tomato ketchup
4 tbsp black treacle
2 tbsp soft dark brown sugar
2 tsp salt
¼ tsp pepper
325 ml/11 fl oz pale ale
2 tbsp cider vinegar or red wine vinegar
2 tbsp Worcestershire sauce
3 red, green or mixed jalapeño chillies, chopped

1. Heat the oil in a saucepan over a medium–high heat. Add the onion and fry for 3–5 minutes, or until soft. Add the chilli powder and cayenne pepper, then stir for 30 seconds. Add the remaining ingredients, except the chillies, stirring until the ketchup, treacle and sugar are blended.

2. Bring to the boil, skimming the surface, as necessary. Add the chillies. Reduce the heat and leave to gently bubble, skimming the surface as necessary and stirring occasionally, for about 30 minutes, or until the sauce has a coating consistency.

3. Transfer the sauce to a food processor or blender and purée. Pass the mixture through a sieve, rubbing backwards and forwards with a wooden spoon and scraping the base of the sieve to produce as much purée as possible.

4. The sauce can be used immediately or it can be left to cool completely and stored in an airtight container in the refrigerator for up to 2 weeks. For guidelines on longer storage, see page 10.

TASTEBUDS-ON-FIRE THAI GREEN SAUCE

With this sauce in the fridge, you will be enjoying a delicious curry with all the flavours of Thailand in no time! This sauce is especially good when used in poultry or vegetable curries.

MAKES: ABOUT 350 ML/ 12 FL OZ **PREP TIME: 10 MINS** **COOK TIME: 15 MINS**

INGREDIENTS

2 tbsp sunflower oil

400 ml/14 fl oz canned coconut milk

1 tbsp Thai fish sauce, or to taste

fresh lime juice, to taste

pepper

THAI GREEN CURRY PASTE

6 green bird's eye chillies, stems removed, roughly chopped

4 fresh coriander sprigs

4 spring onions, chopped

2 green serrano chillies, chopped

2 garlic cloves, chopped

2 lemon grass stalks, outer layer removed, chopped

1 kaffir lime leaf, or the finely grated zest of 1 lime

2.5-cm/1-inch piece fresh ginger, chopped

1 tbsp sunflower oil

1 tsp ground coriander

1. To make the green curry paste, put all the ingredients into a food processor or blender and purée until a thick paste forms.

2. Heat the oil in a wok or saucepan over a high heat. Add the curry paste and stir for 4–5 minutes, or until you can smell the aroma.

3. Stir in the coconut milk and fish sauce and season with pepper to taste. Reduce the heat and simmer, stirring occasionally, for 10 minutes until the flavours have blended and the sauce is reduced. Add lime juice, to taste, and adjust the fish sauce and pepper, if needed.

4. The sauce can be used immediately, or left to cool completely and kept in an airtight container in the refrigerator for up to 3 days.

40

RED-HOT GARLIC & CHILLI OIL

Chilli oil can be used to spice up a huge range of dishes, from drizzling over pizzas or pasta to adding a splash to Mexican-style beef chillies. The longer you leave the oil to settle, the hotter it gets!

MAKES: ABOUT 225 ML/ 8 FL OZ **PREP TIME: 5 MINS** **COOK TIME: 2 HRS**

INGREDIENTS

5 garlic cloves, halved lengthways

2 tbsp deseeded and chopped jalapeño chilli

1 tsp dried oregano

225 ml/8 fl oz rapeseed oil

1. Preheat the oven to 150°C/300°F/Gas Mark 2. Combine the garlic, chilli and oregano with the oil in an ovenproof glass measuring jug. Place on a glass pie plate in the centre of the oven and heat for 1½–2 hours. The temperature of the oil should reach 120°C/250°F.

2. Remove from the oven, allow to cool, then strain through muslin into a clean jar. Store in an airtight container in the refrigerator for up to 1 month. You can also leave the garlic and chilli pieces in the oil and strain before using.

HERO TIPS

Be very careful during the heating of the oil stage in Step 1 of this recipe. Make sure to use an ovenproof measuring jug and use thick oven gloves to carefully remove the oil from the oven when it reaches the desired temperature.

FEELING HOT, HOT, HOT!

IT'S GETTING HOT IN HERE!

Chillies can be deceptive little things – and some of the hottest chillies in the world don't look too fierce at all from the outside. Cut them open, however, and a fascinating anatomy is revealed....

CALYX
The structural base of the chilli – and the point from which it flowers on the plant.

PEDUNCLE
Essentially a fancy name for the stalk. You don't eat this bit, obviously!

EXOCARP
The protective layer of skin, or peel, around the chilli.

SEEDS

Contrary to popular myth, these are not the hottest part of the chilli – though their position next to the capsaicin gland (below) means they do absorb much of the heat from there.

PLACENTA

As you might guess by the name, this is the source of the biological growth of the chilli – from the seeds inside to the fruit itself. Depending on the variety of chilli, this can be white, yellow or red.

MESOCARP

This fleshy layer protects the inside of the chilli, and also provides structural support.

CAPSAICIN GLAND

This is where the hotness comes from! Running from the placenta down the length of the chilli, this gland produces capsaicin, the source of all chilli heat.

ENDOCARP

The inside of the chilli. Contains some heat due to its closeness to the capsaicin gland.

CHIPOTLE & LIME INFERNO SAUCE

Morita chipotle chillies and dried red chilli flakes give this sauce a smoky flavour, reminiscent of foods grilled over wood chips, with a good hit of heat. The zingy lime adds a refreshing finish to the strong flavours. This is a good sauce to use in any slow-cooked meat dish.

MAKES: ABOUT 300 ML/ 10 FL OZ

PREP TIME: 10 MINS PLUS MATURING

COOK TIME: 10 MINS

INGREDIENTS

4 tbsp sunflower oil or rapeseed oil

1 white onion, finely chopped

2 large garlic cloves, crushed

1 tsp ground cinnamon

½ tsp ground allspice

½ tsp ground cumin

8 dried chipotle, morita or meco chillies, or a combination, toasted and soaked (see page 82), stems removed and the soaking water reserved

1 tbsp dried red chilli flakes

1 tsp Mexican oregano or dried marjoram

1 tsp dried thyme

finely grated zest of 1 large lime

2 tbsp freshly squeezed lime juice, or to taste

salt and pepper

1. Heat the oil in a frying pan over a medium heat. Add the onion and fry, stirring, for 3–5 minutes, or until soft. Add the garlic, cinnamon, allspice and cumin and fry for a further minute. Transfer to a food processor or blender.

2. Coarsely chop the chillies and add them to the food processor with the chilli flakes, oregano, thyme, and salt and pepper to taste. Purée until a paste forms, scraping down the sides. Add 1–2 tablespoons of the soaking liquid and process until a soft, thick sauce forms.

3. Pour the sauce into the pan and bring to the boil, stirring. Boil for 2–3 minutes, or until thick. Stir in the lime zest and lime juice. Adjust the seasoning, if necessary, and add extra juice, if desired.

4. The sauce is now ready to use, but is best if left to cool completely and stored in an airtight container in the refrigerator for at least 1 day. It will keep for up to 2 weeks in the refrigerator. For guidelines on longer storage, see page 10.

CREOLE GUMBO FLAMIN' SAUCE

Louisiana gumbos can be mild or spicy hot, and this sauce is one for heat lovers. Green Thai chillies are added to the 'holy trinity' of Creole kitchens – celery, onion and green or red peppers – with an extra burst of heat from cayenne pepper.

MAKES: ABOUT 600 ML/ 1 PINT　　**PREP TIME: 10 MINS**　　**COOK TIME: 1¼ HRS**

INGREDIENTS

4 tbsp sunflower oil or corn oil
4 tbsp plain flour
2 celery sticks, finely chopped
1 large onion, finely chopped
1 green pepper, chopped
1 red pepper, chopped
4 large garlic cloves, crushed
2 green Thai chillies, finely chopped
1 tsp cayenne pepper
1 tsp smoked sweet paprika
700 ml/1¼ pints chicken stock
400 g/14 oz canned chopped tomatoes
450 g/1 lb okra, thinly sliced
2 bay leaves
1 tsp salt
1 tsp dried thyme
½ tsp dried marjoram
pinch of pepper
½ tsp Louisiana Hot Pepper Sauce (see page 80) or other hot sauce (optional)

1. Heat the oil in a large saucepan over a medium–high heat. Slowly whisk in the flour, whisking constantly to prevent lumps forming. Cook the mixture, whisking, for about 10 minutes, or until it turns a dark hazelnut colour.

2. Add the celery, onion and green and red peppers, then reduce the heat and stir for 5–8 minutes, or until the vegetables are soft. Stir in the garlic, chillies, cayenne pepper and paprika and cook for a further minute.

3. Add the stock, tomatoes, okra, bay leaves, salt, thyme, marjoram and pepper. Cover and bring to the boil, then reduce the heat and leave to simmer for about 1 hour, or until the sauce thickens. Adjust the pepper, if necessary, and stir in the hot sauce if the sauce isn't fiery enough.

4. The sauce can be used immediately, or left to cool completely and stored in an airtight container in the refrigerator for up to 2 days. This sauce can be frozen for up to 1 month, see page 10.

FEEL-THE-HEAT HARISSA SAUCE

For this sauce, use whatever hot chillies are available – the colour of the sauce will range from flame red to a devilish brownish-red depending on the chillies used. After several days, the covering oil will have absorbed some of the heat and is great for using in salad dressings.

MAKES: ABOUT 175 ML/ 6 FL OZ

PREP TIME: 5 MINS PLUS SOAKING

COOK TIME: 1-2 MINS

INGREDIENTS

12 hot dried red chillies, such as aji, guajillo, New Mexican or pasilla, or a combination

1 tbsp Aleppo chilli flakes

125 ml/4 fl oz olive oil, plus extra, if needed

1 tsp caraway seeds

1 tsp cumin seeds

½ tsp fennel seeds

2 red jalapeño chillies, finely chopped

salt and pepper

1. Put the dried chillies into a heatproof bowl, pour over boiling water to cover and leave to stand for 15 minutes. Drain well and pat dry. When cool enough to handle, remove the stems and finely chop the chillies.

2. Transfer to a bowl and add the chilli flakes and oil. Set aside for 1 hour.

3. Meanwhile, heat a dry frying pan over a medium–high heat. Add the caraway seeds, cumin seeds and fennel seeds and dry-fry for 1–2 minutes, or until aromatic. Tip the seeds out of the pan, then finely grind in a mortar with a pestle.

4. Transfer the soaked chilli mixture, ground seeds and chopped fresh chillies to a small food processor or blender. Season to taste, then purée. Adjust the seasoning, if necessary. Slowly add more oil, if necessary, to make a thick sauce.

5. The sauce can be used immediately, or stored, with a layer of olive oil poured over the surface, in an airtight container in the refrigerator for up to 2 weeks.

INTENSE TEXAN CHILLI SAUCE

Texan chilli – or Big Red as the locals know it – is not made with beans, just meat, so it needs a tasty sauce like this with plenty of heat and flavour. This sauce can also be used in other chilli recipes that are made with kidney beans and vegetables.

MAKES: ABOUT 700 ML/ 1¼ PINTS

PREP TIME: 10 MINS

COOK TIME: 30 MINS

INGREDIENTS

2 tbsp sunflower oil or rapeseed oil

1 red onion, chopped

2 large garlic cloves, chopped

1 green serrano chilli, halved lengthways

1 tbsp soft dark brown sugar

2 tsp ground cumin

2 tsp dried Mexican oregano or dried thyme

2 dried morita chipotle chillies, toasted, soaked, deseeded and chopped (see page 82)

1 dried guajillo chilli, toasted, soaked, deseeded and chopped (see page 82)

1 dried New Mexico red chilli, toasted, soaked, deseeded and chopped (see page 82)

400 g/14 oz canned chopped tomatoes

125 ml/4 fl oz beef stock

125 ml/4 fl oz strong black coffee

salt and pepper

1. Heat the oil in a saucepan over a medium–high heat. Add the onion and fry for 3–5 minutes, or until soft. Add the garlic, serrano chilli, sugar, cumin and oregano and fry for a further minute.

2. Transfer the onion mixture to a food processor or blender. Add the chipotle chillies, guajillo chilli and New Mexico chilli, tomatoes, stock and coffee and season to taste with salt and pepper. Process until puréed, scraping down the sides as necessary.

3. Transfer the purée to the pan and bring to the boil. Reduce the heat to low, cover and simmer for 15 minutes, stirring occasionally. Adjust the seasoning, if necessary.

4. The sauce can be used immediately, or left to cool completely and stored in an airtight container in the refrigerator for up to 3 days. This sauce can be frozen for up to 3 months, see page 10.

CHIMICHURRI SWELTERING SAUCE

No Latin American barbecue is complete without a bowl of zingy, fresh chimichurri, a blend of herbs and chillies. This hot and spicy version has a bird's eye chilli to crank up the heat. Serve with all grilled and roasted meats or serve with a selection of crudités.

MAKES: ABOUT 175 ML/ 6 FL OZ

PREP TIME: 5 MINS PLUS MARINATING

COOK TIME: NONE

INGREDIENTS
30 g/1 oz fresh coriander leaves

30 g/1 oz fresh flat-leaf parsley leaves

4 garlic cloves, roughly chopped

1–2 green bird's eye chillies, finely chopped

1 tsp dried chilli flakes

1 tsp dried Mexican oregano or 1 tsp dried thyme (optional)

125 ml/4 fl oz sunflower oil or rapeseed oil

4 tbsp red wine vinegar or white wine vinegar

salt and pepper

1. Put the coriander, parsley, garlic, chillies, chilli flakes, oregano, if using, and salt and pepper to taste into a food processor and finely chop, scraping down the sides, as necessary. Do not blend to a purée.

2. With the motor running, slowly drizzle in the oil. Add the vinegar and adjust the seasoning, if necessary.

3. The sauce can be used immediately, but is best if stored in an airtight container in the refrigerator for at least 3 hours to allow the flavours to blend. The sauce will keep for up to 3 days in the refrigerator if covered with an extra layer of oil, although its bright green colour will dull. Pour off the oil before serving.

HERO TIPS

If you don't want to use a food processor, finely chop the coriander, parsley and garlic, then mix together in a non-metallic bowl.

RED-HOT GREEN SAUCE

Tortilla chips with ready-made salsa will seem mild and boring once you've tried this sauce that's packed full of punch with pickled jalapeños and hot smoked paprika! It's zesty and hot and the fresh green colour looks appetizing in a contrasting bowl.

MAKES: ABOUT 400 ML/ 14 FL OZ **PREP TIME: 10 MINS** **COOK TIME: NONE**

INGREDIENTS

450 g/1 lb canned tomatillos, drained, stem ends removed and roughly chopped

4 spring onions, chopped

2 large garlic cloves, roughly chopped

2 tbsp drained pickled jalapeño chillies, chopped

handful of coriander leaves

freshly squeezed lime juice, to taste

clear honey, to taste

½ tsp hot smoked paprika

salt and pepper

finely chopped coriander, to garnish

1. Put the tomatillos, spring onions, garlic, chillies and coriander leaves into a food processor and process in short blasts to finely chop, but not purée.

2. Transfer the mixture to a bowl. Season to taste with salt and pepper, then add lime juice and honey to taste. Stir in the paprika.

3. The sauce can be used immediately, or stored in an airtight container in the refrigerator for up to 4 days, although the colour will start to dull after 3 days. Sprinkle with chopped coriander just before serving.

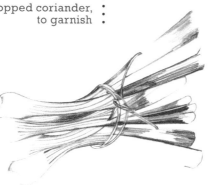

SPICE UP YOUR LIFE!

Chillies are only one way to add heat to your food. Why not check out some of these other spices and pastes that flavour hot sauce recipes around the globe?

HARISSA PASTE

Seemingly endless variations exist for this dark red paste that adds heat and flavour to food in North Africa. The constant ingredients are chillies, oil and caraway seeds. Make your own (see page 52) or buy it in supermarkets or Middle Eastern food shops.

HORSERADISH

This thick, white root has an intense, sharp and hot flavour when it is freshly grated. Mixing grated horseradish with lemon juice helps prolong the sharpness. If buying grated horseradish, avoid horseradish sauce, which is mixed with cream, or grated horseradish in vinegar.

MUSTARD

Choose dried bright yellow mustard powder for the hottest flavour in a sauce. To avoid lumps forming, treat it like flour and stir any liquids into it.

PAPRIKA

Produced in Hungary, but also in Spain and many other countries, paprika is the finely ground powder of sweet peppers. Its heat ranges from mild and sweet to intensely hot. Spanish pimentón is paprika made from dried and smoked peppers.

SAMBAL OELEK PASTE

From South-east Asia, this red sauce, made with chillies, salt and citrus juice or vinegar, comes in varying degrees of hotness. It is sold in supermarkets and specialist food shops.

SZECHUAN PEPPERCORNS

The flavour of these rosy-brown dried peppercorns is unmistakable – the heat blends with a lingering tingling sensation on your tongue and cheeks.

WASABI

Known as Japanese horseradish, pale green wasabi comes from a root and packs quite a punch. It is pungent and hot, and sold ready-made as a paste or in powder form.

61

TRY-IT-IF-YOU-DARE THAI RED CURRY SAUCE

Although ready-made red curry pastes are bright red, the home-made pastes tend to be much paler in colour. This recipe includes Kashmiri chilli powder or hot paprika, as much for the redness they impart as their heat.

MAKES: ABOUT 450 ML/ 16 FL OZ   **PREP TIME: 30 MINS**   **COOK TIME: 10 MINS**

INGREDIENTS
2 tbsp sunflower oil

400 ml/14 fl oz coconut milk

1 tbsp Thai fish sauce, or to taste

1 tbsp freshly squeezed lime juice, or to taste

1 tbsp dark soy sauce, or to taste

4 fresh red or green Thai chillies, thinly sliced

pepper

RED CURRY PASTE
24 dried bird's eye chillies, stems removed

2 large garlic cloves, chopped

2 large shallots, chopped

1 lemon grass stalk, chopped

2.5-cm/1-inch piece galangal, coarsely chopped

2.5-cm/1-inch piece fresh ginger, finely chopped

2 tsp Kashmiri chilli powder or hot paprika

2 tsp ground coriander

1 tsp ground cumin

1. To make the curry paste, soak the chillies in hot water to cover for 20 minutes, or until soft, weighing them down with a small heatproof plate.

2. Strain, reserving the liquid, then chop the chillies and put them into a small food processor.

3. Add the remaining paste ingredients and purée, scraping down the sides and adding a little of the reserved liquid, as necessary, until a thick paste forms.

4. Heat the oil in a wok over a high heat. Add 3 tablespoons of the curry paste and stir for 30 seconds. Stir in the coconut milk, fish sauce, lime juice, soy sauce and pepper to taste and bring to the boil, stirring. Reduce the heat and simmer for 5 minutes. Stir in the chillies. Adjust the curry paste, fish sauce, lime juice, soy sauce and pepper to taste.

5. The sauce can be used immediately, or left to cool completely and stored in an airtight container in the refrigerator for up to 3 days.

SEARING SERRANO & CORIANDER SAUCE

This can be made either smooth, like mayonnaise, in a food processor, or chunkier, like guacamole, by hand. Either way, it's great for adding a kick to pan-fried seafood or used instead of guacamole in tacos and burritos.

MAKES: ABOUT 225 ML/ 8 FL OZ   **PREP TIME: 10 MINS**   **COOK TIME: NONE**

INGREDIENTS
5 tbsp sunflower oil

3 tbsp freshly squeezed lime juice, or to taste

1 tsp clear honey, or to taste

125 g/4½ oz soft, ripe avocado, roughly chopped

2 red or green Serrano chillies, deseeded and roughly chopped

1-cm/½-inch piece fresh ginger, finely grated

small handful coriander leaves, roughly chopped

salt and pepper

1. Blend 3 tablespoons of the oil, the lime juice, honey, and salt and pepper to taste in a small food processor. Add the avocado and the remaining oil and process until blended, scraping down the sides as necessary.

2. Add the chillies, ginger and coriander leaves to the food processor and process, in short blasts, until the chillies and coriander are finely chopped and distributed through the sauce.

3. Alternatively, whisk together 3 tablespoons of the oil, the lime juice, honey, and salt and pepper to taste in a non-metallic bowl. Use a fork to mash in the avocado, then beat in the chillies, ginger, coriander and the remaining oil.

4. Adjust the seasoning, adding more honey or lime juice to taste. Serve immediately.

HERO TIPS

Unlike most hot sauces, this sauce is best eaten immediately, as the colour darkens within 30 minutes of preparation.

FIERY & FIERCE GOCHUJANG SAUCE

Korean cooks used to make enough gochujang, a fermented chilli and soybean paste, in the spring to last a family throughout the year. Use this sauce as a marinade or dipping sauce or for basting meat and poultry as they cook.

MAKES: ABOUT 150 ML/ 5 FL OZ   **PREP TIME: 5 MINS**   **COOK TIME: NONE**

INGREDIENTS

5 tbsp gochujang paste
2 tsp chilli paste
2 tbsp sugar
2 tbsp hot water
2 tsp light soy sauce
1 tsp rice vinegar
1 tsp toasted sesame oil

1. Combine the gochujang paste, chilli paste and sugar in a heatproof bowl, then add the water, stirring to blend and dissolve the sugar and paste.

2. Stir in the soy sauce, vinegar and sesame oil. Leave to cool completely.

3. The sauce can be used immediately, or stored in an airtight container in the refrigerator for up to 2 weeks. If you want to make larger quantities, see page 10 for guidelines on longer storage.

HERO TIPS

This recipe combines authentic flavour with the speed of using the fermented bean and chilli paste that is sold in plastic tubs in many Asian supermarkets. No Korean barbecue or bibimbap is complete without it!

NOT-FOR-THE-FAINT-HEARTED NACHO SAUCE

This nacho sauce is creamy and smooth with layers of heat from mustard powder, hot sauce and finely chopped chillies. For nachos with heat, top tortilla chips with this sauce. It is also great mixed with cooked pasta or spooned over jacket potatoes.

MAKES: ABOUT 300 ML/ 10 FL OZ   **PREP TIME: 5 MINS**   **COOK TIME: 15 MINS**

INGREDIENTS

125 g/4½ oz mature Cheddar cheese, coarsely grated

3 tbsp cornflour

1 tbsp mustard powder

250 ml/9 fl oz milk

2 tbsp cream cheese

2 tsp Louisiana Hot Pepper Sauce (see page 80), Spicy Sriracha Sauce (see page 92) or other hot sauce, to taste

2 red or green jalapeño chillies, finely chopped

salt and pepper

1. Mix together the cheese, cornflour and mustard powder in a heatproof bowl, then set aside.

2. Put the milk into a saucepan and bring just to the boil. Stir 4 tablespoons of the hot milk into the cheese mixture, stirring until well blended. Add the cheese mixture to the milk, whisking vigorously.

3. Return the mixture just to the boil, then reduce the heat and simmer, whisking frequently, for 5 minutes until the cheese has melted and the sauce is smooth and has reduced. Remove the pan from the heat and stir in the cream cheese and hot sauce. Season to taste, then stir in the chillies.

4. The sauce can be used immediately, or left to cool completely and stored in an airtight container in the refrigerator for up to 3 days. To serve, reheat gently without boiling.

HERO TIPS Do not add the cornflour or the mustard powder directly to the hot milk or lumps will form. Whisk vigorously to ensure a smooth mixture.

SCORCHING MOLE SAUCE

Toasted nuts and seeds make this classic Mexican sauce as rich as it is hot. The mix of pasilla and ancho chillies gives a deep flavour that supports the heat. It's the chocolate, however, that is the essential ingredient in terms of its distinctive flavour.

MAKES: ABOUT 350 ML/ 12 FL OZ   **PREP TIME: 15 MINS**   **COOK TIME: 10 MINS**

INGREDIENTS

3 tbsp rapeseed oil or sunflower oil

1 tbsp shelled pumpkin seeds

1 day-old soft flour tortilla, broken into small pieces

1 red onion, chopped

1 tsp ground cinnamon

½ tsp cayenne pepper

½ tsp ground coriander

½ tsp ground cumin

¼ tsp ground cloves

3 dried pasilla chillies, toasted, soaked, stems and seeds removed (see page 82)

1 dried ancho chilli, toasted, soaked, stem and seeds removed (see page 82)

4 tbsp blanched almonds, toasted

4 tbsp peeled hazelnuts, toasted

2 tsp sesame seeds, toasted

30 g/1 oz plain chocolate, at least 70 per cent cocoa solids, chopped

salt and pepper

1. Heat 1 tablespoon of the oil in a frying pan over a medium–high heat. Add the pumpkin seeds and fry for 30–60 seconds, or until they start popping. Transfer to a food processor or blender.

2. Heat another tablespoon of oil in the pan and quickly fry the tortilla pieces, for 1 minute, or until golden. Add to the food processor.

3. Heat the remaining oil in the pan. Add the onion and fry for 3–5 minutes, or until soft. Add the spices and fry for a further minute.

4. Add the onion mixture to the food processor with the pasilla chillies, ancho chilli, nuts, sesame seeds and chocolate and season to taste with salt and pepper. Process the sauce, scraping down the sides, as necessary, until a thick, grainy sauce forms. Adjust the seasoning, if necessary.

5. The sauce can be used immediately, or left to cool completely and stored in an airtight container in the refrigerator for up to 3 days. This sauce can be frozen for up to 1 month, see page 10.

VOLATILE TERIYAKI SAUCE

Fiery green wasabi paste, known as Japanese horseradish, and fresh ginger give this traditional Japanese sauce a burst of heat, as well as extra flavour.

MAKES: ABOUT 75 ML/ 2½ FL OZ　　　**PREP TIME: 5 MINS**　　　**COOK TIME: 8-10 MINS**

INGREDIENTS

125 ml/4 fl oz Japanese soy sauce
4 tbsp sake
4 tbsp mirin or dry sherry
4 tbsp soft brown sugar
1 garlic clove, crushed
2.5-cm/1-inch piece fresh ginger
1 tbsp green wasabi paste, or to taste

1. Combine the soy sauce, sake, mirin, sugar and garlic in a saucepan, stirring to dissolve the sugar. Grate the ginger directly into the pan to capture all the juices. Bring to the boil, then reduce the heat and simmer, uncovered, for 8–10 minutes, or until thickened to a coating consistency.

2. Add the wasabi paste and stir until dissolved.

3. The sauce can be used immediately, or left to cool completely and stored in an airtight container in the refrigerator for up to 3 weeks. Grate in the ginger only when you are ready to serve, then reheat the sauce.

INCANDESCENT CURRY SAUCE

This is a good sauce to make in large batches and freeze in convenient portions for future meals. This sauce is versatile enough to be used as the base for meat, poultry and vegetable curries.

MAKES: ABOUT 400 ML/ 14 FL OZ **PREP TIME: 10 MINS** **COOK TIME: 20 MINS**

INGREDIENTS
400 g/14 oz canned chopped tomatoes

2–3 green or red bird's eye chillies, to taste, chopped

4 garlic cloves, chopped

1-cm/½-inch piece fresh ginger, chopped

3 tbsp groundnut oil or sunflower oil

2 onions, finely chopped

1½ tsp salt

½ tsp turmeric

pinch of soft light brown sugar

1 tbsp garam masala

pepper

1. Put the tomatoes, chillies, garlic and ginger into a food processor or blender and purée. Alternatively, pound together the chillies, garlic and ginger with a pestle and mortar, then pound in the tomatoes. Set aside.

2. Heat the oil in a large wok or saucepan over a medium–high heat. Add the onions and fry, stirring constantly, for 5–8 minutes, or until lightly coloured. Add the tomato mixture and bring to the boil, stirring.

3. Stir in the salt, turmeric and sugar and season to taste with pepper. Reduce the heat to very low and leave to simmer, uncovered, for 10–15 minutes, or until the oil separates around the edge of the sauce.

4. Stir in the garam masala and remove the sauce from the heat.

5. The sauce can be used immediately, or left to cool completely and stored in an airtight container in the refrigerator for up to 3 days. This sauce can be frozen for up to 3 months, see page 10.

BLOW YOUR HEAD OFF!

PERI-PERI AT YOUR PERIL SAUCE

This peri-peri sauce is as good as any you would find at well-known restaurants! Pair this sauce with fried chicken wings for a hot and spicy meal.

MAKES: ABOUT 75 ML/ 2½ FL OZ   **PREP TIME: 10 MINS**   **COOK TIME: 10 MINS**

INGREDIENTS

4 tbsp sunflower oil

24 peri-peri chillies or red bird's eye chillies, chopped

½ onion, finely chopped

4 large garlic cloves, chopped

1 tsp sweet paprika

¼ tsp ground allspice

6 tbsp freshly squeezed lemon juice, or to taste

2 tbsp water

finely grated zest of 1 lemon

salt and pepper

1. Turn the extractor to high or open a window to allow air to circulate. Heat the oil in a saucepan over a medium heat. Add the chillies and onion and fry for 3 minutes. Add the garlic, paprika and allspice and stir for a further minute.

2. Add 4 tablespoons of the lemon juice and the water and season to taste with salt and pepper. Bring to the boil, stirring. Reduce the heat to very low, cover and simmer for 5 minutes, or until the chillies are very soft. Uncover and check once or twice to make sure the garlic doesn't burn.

3. If you would like a smooth, restaurant-style sauce, transfer the ingredients to a small food processor or blender and purée or leave as a chunky sauce, if preferred. Stir in the remaining lemon juice. Adjust the seasoning and lemon juice, as desired. Stir in the lemon zest.

4. The sauce can be used immediately, or left to cool completely and stored in an airtight container in the refrigerator for up to 2 weeks. For guidelines on longer storage, see page 10.

JAMAICAN JERK SIZZLING SAUCE

This hot, hot, hot Caribbean favourite can be used as a marinade or as a basting sauce while barbecuing. Chicken is its traditional partner, but it also adds a sunny Caribbean taste to most meat and seafood dishes.

MAKES: ABOUT 300 ML/ 10 FL OZ

PREP TIME: 10 MINS PLUS RESTING

COOK TIME: NONE

INGREDIENTS

4 tbsp freshly squeezed lemon juice

4 tbsp dark soy sauce

4 tbsp sunflower oil

4 tbsp red wine vinegar or white wine vinegar

4 red Scotch bonnet chillies or habanero chillies, deseeded and very finely chopped

4 spring onions, very finely chopped

1 shallot, very finely chopped

2.5-cm/1-inch piece fresh ginger, grated

2 tbsp soft light brown sugar

2 tsp dried thyme

1 tsp ground allspice

½ tsp ground cinnamon

¼ tsp ground cloves

salt and pepper

1. Mix together the lemon juice, soy sauce, oil and vinegar in a large non-metallic bowl.

2. Stir in the remaining ingredients and season to taste with salt and pepper, stirring until the sugar dissolves. Set aside for at least 30 minutes for the flavours to blend.

3. The sauce can be used immediately, or stored in an airtight container in the refrigerator for up to 1 month.

LOUISIANA HOT PEPPER SAUCE

This sauce is traditionally made with fresh, small tabasco chillies but they can be difficult to source, so dried cayenne or bird's eye chillies are used in this recipe to give the same tongue-tingling sensation.

MAKES: ABOUT 125 ML/ 4 FL OZ

PREP TIME: 5 MINS PLUS SOAKING

COOK TIME: 15 MINS

INGREDIENTS

55 g/2 oz dried red cayenne peppers or dried red bird's eye chillies, stems removed, very roughly chopped and soaked for 30 minutes (see page 82)

125 ml/4 fl oz white wine vinegar

½ tsp salt

1. Turn the extractor to high or open a window. Drain the soaked chillies. Put the chillies, vinegar and salt into a small saucepan. Cover the pan and bring to the boil, then reduce the heat to low and leave to simmer for 10–12 minutes, or until very soft.

2. Tip the contents of the pan into a small food processor or blender and purée, scraping down the sides, as necessary. Strain the blended mixture to remove the seeds. Transfer the sauce to a non-metallic bowl and leave to cool completely.

3. Leave the sauce to mature for at least 2 weeks in an airtight container in the refrigerator before using. The sauce will then keep in the refrigerator for a further month. For longer storage, see page 10.

ROASTING HOT CARIBBEAN SAUCE

Hot, hot, hot – hotter than the Caribbean sun! There are many recipes for hot sauces throughout the Caribbean and this version is inspired by the pepper sauces from Trinidad. Use it as a marinade for barbecued and grilled food or stir into soups and stews for a chilli sensation.

MAKES: ABOUT 300 ML/ 10 FL OZ　　**PREP TIME: 10 MINS**　　**COOK TIME: 10 MINS**

INGREDIENTS
8 red and/or orange Scotch bonnet chillies or habanero chillies, deseeded
4 garlic cloves, finely chopped
1 carrot, sliced
1 onion, finely chopped
6 tbsp cider vinegar or red wine vinegar
1 tbsp freshly squeezed orange juice or lime juice, or to taste
salt and pepper

1. Bring a small saucepan of lightly salted water to the boil. Add the chillies and blanch for 30 seconds, or until just soft. Use a slotted spoon to transfer them to a blender or food processor.

2. Return the water to the boil. Add the garlic, carrot and onion and boil for 5–8 minutes, or until the carrot is very soft. Drain the vegetables and add to the blender with the vinegar, orange juice, and salt and pepper to taste.

3. Purée the ingredients until a sauce forms. Pass the sauce through a fine sieve into a bowl, rubbing backwards and forwards with a wooden spoon and scraping the base of the sieve to produce as much purée as possible. Adjust the seasoning, if necessary. Transfer to a bowl and leave to cool completely.

4. Leave the sauce to mature in an airtight container in the refrigerator for 2 weeks, shaking it occasionally. It will keep for a further 2 weeks in the refrigerator. For guidelines on longer storage, see page 10.

TOAST IT!

Not all chillies are best eaten fresh! Dried chillies are often toasted before using to intensify their flavours... and they can also be soaked to soften before blending. Both techniques are easy and well worth investigating.

TOASTING CHILLIES

Heat a dry frying pan over a medium heat. Add the dry chillies and fry until you can smell their aroma. Press large chillies, such as guajillos and pastillas, with a metal spatula against the hot surface until they slightly puff up and soften. Immediately remove them from the pan and set aside. Take care not to over-toast them or they will taste bitter.

Smaller chillies, such as pequin, should be stirred constantly so they don't burn.

Alternatively, put the chillies on a baking tray and place in a preheated 220°C/425°F/Gas Mark 7 oven for 5 minutes, or until they slightly puff up and soften.

SOAKING CHILLIES

Many recipes specify to soak chillies so they are soft enough to blend. Put them in a heatproof bowl and pour over enough boiling water to cover. Leave to stand for 5 minutes, or until softened and flexible. Smaller chillies, such as bird's eyes and chipotles, need to be weighted down with a small saucepan lid or heatproof plate to keep them submerged.

Strain the chillies well, then pat dry and remove the stalks. Some recipes also suggest cutting the chillies open and removing the seeds.

TOASTING NUTS & SEEDS

Intensify the flavour of nuts and seeds by dry-frying them in a heavy-based pan, stirring constantly, until they turn golden brown. Watch closely because they can burn in the blink of an eye. As soon as you can smell the aroma, immediately tip them out of the pan so the oils do not continue cooking and develop a bitter flavour.

TOP TIPS FOR TOASTING & SOAKING

• Save on washing up – when a recipe specifies to toast and soak chillies, dry-fry them, then add water to the pan and bring to the boil. Turn off the heat and leave the chillies to soak until they soften.

• Never throw away the liquid you soak your chillies in. It's full of flavour and is great for giving a kick to soups, stews and gravies. Leave it to cool, then transfer to an airtight container and store in the fridge. Or, for the really organized, freeze in an ice-cube tray, then transfer the individual cubes to a freezerproof bag.

• To save time when cooking, toast batches of chillies, nuts and seeds and store them individually in airtight containers, ready to use next time.

DANGEROUS ADOBO SAUCE

Chipotle chillies are dried jalapeño chillies available in two forms, morita or meco, both of which can be used in this recipe. Meco chipotles give a smokier flavour that goes particularly well with slow-cooked meat dishes.

MAKES: ABOUT 300 ML/ 10 FL OZ   **PREP TIME: 10 MINS**   **COOK TIME: 1½-1¾ HRS**

INGREDIENTS

- 4 tbsp tomato purée
- 600 ml/1 pint water
- 6 tbsp white wine vinegar
- 12 dried chipotle chillies, stems removed
- 4 garlic cloves, crushed
- ½ red onion, very finely chopped
- 2 tbsp soft light brown sugar
- 1 tbsp ground cumin
- 1 tbsp dried Mexican oregano or dried thyme
- 2 tsp hot smoked paprika
- 2 tsp cayenne pepper
- ½ tsp salt
- pepper

1. Dissolve the tomato purée in the water and vinegar in a deep saucepan. Stir in the remaining ingredients and season with pepper to taste. Cover and bring to the boil.

2. Uncover, reduce the heat to very low and simmer for 1¼–1½ hours, or until the chillies are very soft and the sauce thickens.

3. Transfer the sauce to a blender or food processor and purée. Strain the sauce through a sieve into a bowl, rubbing backwards and forwards with a wooden spoon and scraping the base of the sieve to produce as much purée as possible. Set aside to cool completely.

4. The sauce can be used immediately, or stored in an airtight container in the refrigerator for up to 3 weeks. For guidelines on longer storage, see page 10.

BLISTERING BLACK BEAN SAUCE

The Szechuan peppercorns in this stir-fry sauce will produce a distinctive tingling sensation in your mouth. Look for the peppercorns, as well as the black beans, in Chinese food stores. Don't confuse these salty beans with the ones used in Caribbean and Latin American cooking.

MAKES: ABOUT 150 ML/ 5 FL OZ　　**PREP TIME: 10 MINS**　　**COOK TIME: 5 MINS**

INGREDIENTS

2 tbsp groundnut oil or sunflower oil

55 g/2 oz salted or fermented black beans

4 spring onions, finely chopped

4 green Thai chillies, finely chopped

1 tbsp Szechuan peppercorns, toasted and crushed

1-cm/½-inch piece fresh ginger, finely grated

125 ml/4 fl oz beef stock, chicken stock or vegetable stock

4 tbsp light soy sauce

1 tbsp arrowroot, dissolved in 1 tbsp water

1 tsp toasted sesame oil

pepper

1. Heat a wok over a high heat. Add the oil and heat until very hot. Add the beans, spring onions, chillies, peppercorns and ginger and stir-fry for 2 minutes, using a wooden spoon to break up the beans.

2. Add the stock and soy sauce and season with pepper. Bring to the boil, stirring, then reduce the heat to low.

3. Stir in the arrowroot mixture and simmer, without boiling, for 1–2 minutes, or until the sauce is thick and shiny. Adjust the pepper, if necessary. Sprinkle with the sesame oil.

4. The sauce can be used immediately, or it can be left to cool completely and stored, with a thin layer of oil poured over the top, in an airtight container in the refrigerator for up to 1 week.

HERO TIPS

Use 1–2 tablespoons of the black bean sauce per portion of stir-fry. The sauce is especially good in a beef stir-fry with green peppers and mushrooms.

LONE STAR PERILOUS PEQUIN SAUCE

Texans take their hot sauces seriously and this isn't a sauce for the faint-hearted. The native pequin chillies grow to less than 2.5 cm/1 inch and are available all year round as small, rosy-red dried chillies. What they lack in size, they make up for in intense, searing heat.

MAKES: ABOUT 600 ML/ 1 PINT   **PREP TIME: 10 MINS**   **COOK TIME: 40 MINS**

INGREDIENTS

1½ tbsp dried pequin chillies
1 tsp cumin seeds, toasted
½ tsp coriander seeds, toasted
4 tomatoes, about 400 g/14 oz, chopped
1 red onion, chopped
225 ml/8 fl oz passata
4 tbsp red wine vinegar
1 tbsp black treacle
2 tsp dried thyme
salt and pepper

1. Heat a frying pan over a high heat. Add the chillies and dry-fry, stirring, for 30–60 seconds, or until they start to colour. Immediately tip them out of the pan. If they burn they will taste bitter. Use a pestle and mortar or the back of a wooden spoon to finely crush the chillies and seeds.

2. Put the remaining ingredients in a saucepan, add the crushed chillies and season to taste with salt and pepper. Bring to the boil, stirring to dissolve the treacle. Reduce the heat to low, partially cover and simmer for 30 minutes, stirring occasionally to prevent the sauce sticking to the base of the pan.

3. Transfer the sauce to a food processor or blender and purée. Adjust the seasoning, if necessary.

4. The sauce can be used immediately, or left to cool completely and stored in an airtight container in the refrigerator for up to 1 week. This sauce can be frozen for up to 3 months, see page 10.

VOLCANIC VINDALOO SAUCE

This blisteringly hot sauce derives from when the Portuguese introduced the hot chilli and vinegar to Goa in the 16th century. If there is time, leave the masala and crushed chilli mixture to infuse for up to 4 hours in Step 2 for the flavours to intensify.

MAKES: ABOUT 450 ML/ 16 FL OZ   **PREP TIME: 15 MINS**   **COOK TIME: 35 MINS**

INGREDIENTS
2 tbsp sunflower oil
1 onion, thinly sliced
4 large tomatoes, chopped
1 tbsp dark brown sugar
1 tsp salt
125 ml/4 fl oz water
pepper

VINDALOO MASALA
2.5-cm/1-inch cinnamon stick
1½ tsp coriander seeds
½ tsp cumin seeds
½ tsp black mustard seeds
¼ tsp fennel seeds
¼ tsp black peppercorns
2 tbsp red wine vinegar
2.5-cm/1-inch piece fresh ginger, grated
5 dried red Thai chillies or cayenne chillies, finely chopped
2 large garlic cloves, crushed

1. To make the masala, heat a dry frying pan over a medium–high heat. Add the cinnamon, all the seeds and the peppercorns and fry, stirring, for 1–2 minutes until aromatic. Immediately tip out of the pan and finely grind in a small food processor or using a pestle and mortar.

2. Transfer the crushed mixture to a non-metallic bowl, stir in the vinegar, ginger, chillies and garlic and set aside.

3. Heat the oil in a heavy-based saucepan over a low heat. Add the onion and fry for 8–10 minutes, or until lightly browned.

4. Add the tomatoes, sugar, salt, masala mixture and water and stir. Bring to the boil, then reduce the heat to low. Cover and simmer for 15 minutes, stirring occasionally to break down the tomatoes. Season to taste with pepper.

5. The sauce can be used immediately, or left to cool completely and stored in an airtight container in the refrigerator for up to 1 week.

SPICY SRIRACHA SAUCE

Home-made sriracha will never taste exactly the same as the shop-bought variety, because it contains no commercial stabilizers. However, this Thai-style favourite, thickened with a little arrowroot, has a delicious flavour with just the same chilli hit.

MAKES: ABOUT 175 ML/ 6 FL OZ   **PREP TIME: 10 MINS PLUS STANDING**   **COOK TIME: 30 MINS**

INGREDIENTS

14 red jalapeño, serrano or Fresno chillies, or a combination, about 225 g/8 oz total weight, stems removed and halved lengthways

1 red bird's eye chilli, deseeded

8 garlic cloves, coarsely chopped

3 tbsp soft light brown sugar

2 tbsp granulated sugar

2 tsp salt

6 tbsp white wine vinegar

1 tsp arrowroot

1. Put all the ingredients, except the vinegar and arrowroot, into a food processor or blender and finely chop. Transfer to a screw-topped jar large enough to hold the mixture with space at the top and seal. Leave to stand at warm room temperature, shaking once a day, for 2–4 days, or until the mixture becomes liquid.

2. Return the mixture to the food processor, add the vinegar and purée. Strain into a saucepan, rubbing backwards and forwards with a spoon and scraping the sieve to produce as much purée as possible.

3. Turn the extractor to high, or open a window to allow air to circulate. Place the pan over a medium heat, bring the purée to the boil and stir, until it is reduced by a quarter. Reduce the heat to low.

4. Dissolve the arrowroot with 1 tablespoon of the hot liquid, then stir it into the pan. Stir for 30 seconds, until the sauce thickens slightly. Set aside.

5. Allow to cool then leave to mature for 2 weeks in an airtight container in the refrigerator. The sauce will keep for 1 month in the refrigerator. For guidelines on longer storage, see page 10.

FIERY GARLIC-PEPPER SAUCE

This sauce is ideal for adding punchy heat to slow-roasted pork belly, but is equally good in stir-fries and for brushing on chops or steaks before chargrilling.

MAKES: ABOUT 175 ML/ 6 FL OZ **PREP TIME: 5 MINS** **COOK TIME: 1 HR**

INGREDIENTS

10 red bird's eye chillies

2 red peppers, quartered and deseeded

1 garlic bulb, about 12 cloves, separated

½ onion, chopped

1 tsp Chinese five spice

2 tbsp sunflower oil

salt and pepper

1. Preheat the oven to 220°C/425°F/Gas Mark 7.

2. Put the chillies, red peppers, garlic and onion into a shallow ovenproof dish that holds them quite snugly. Sprinkle with the five spice, and salt and pepper to taste, then spoon over the oil and stir into the other ingredients. Cover the dish tightly with foil.

3. Place in the preheated oven and roast for 1 hour, or until all the vegetables are very tender.

4. Tip the vegetables and any cooking juices into a food processor or blender and purée. Pass the mixture through a fine sieve, rubbing backwards and forwards with a wooden spoon and scraping the base of the sieve to produce as much purée as possible. Adjust the salt and pepper, if necessary.

5. The sauce can be used immediately, or stored in an airtight container in the refrigerator for up to 2 weeks. For guidelines on longer storage, see page 10.

HOT-BLOODED HUNGARIAN PAPRIKASH SAUCE

Hungarians fortify themselves against cold winters with spicy-hot meat stews, flavoured with paprika. It comes in varying degrees of heat – this is the searing-hot variety. For a quick taste of Hungary, pour this sauce over cooked chicken thighs and leave to simmer so the flavours blend.

MAKES: ABOUT 350 ML/ 12 FL OZ   **PREP TIME: 10 MINS**   **COOK TIME: 25 MINS**

INGREDIENTS
1 tsp caraway seeds
2 tbsp sunflower oil
1 large onion, thinly sliced
2 tbsp hot Hungarian paprika
300 ml/10 fl oz soured cream
1 tbsp tomato purée
1 tsp dried dill
salt and pepper

1. Toast the caraway seeds in a dry frying pan over a medium–high heat for 1–2 minutes, or until aromatic. Tip them out of the pan into a bowl.

2. Add the oil to the pan and heat. Add the onion and fry for 3–5 minutes, or until soft. Stir in the paprika and cook for 30 seconds.

3. Stir in the soured cream and tomato purée and season to taste with salt and pepper. Bring just to the boil, then reduce the heat to low and simmer for 10–15 minutes, stirring occasionally, until reduced. Stir in the caraway seeds and dill and adjust the seasoning, if necessary.

4. The sauce can be used immediately, or left to cool completely and stored in an airtight container in the refrigerator for up to 3 days.

HERO TIPS
If the sauce thickens too much in the refrigerator, it can be thinned with a little chicken stock when added to meat and vegetables.

HOTTER-THAN-AN-OVEN HABANERO SAUCE

Don't be deceived by the initial sweet flavour. As this sauce hits the back of the tongue, the searing heat kicks in. Typical of many sauces from the Caribbean, this version mixes tropical fruit with habanero or Scotch bonnet chillies. Drizzle over freshly grilled seafood kebabs!

MAKES: ABOUT 175 ML/ 6 FL OZ **PREP TIME: 10 MINS** **COOK TIME: 25 MINS**

INGREDIENTS

8 green habanero or Scotch bonnet chillies, halved, 4 deseeded

2 large green peppers, halved and deseeded

3 tbsp chopped fresh mango

1 white onion, finely chopped

4 tbsp sugar dissolved in 4 tbsp white wine vinegar

2.5-cm/1-inch piece fresh ginger, grated

salt and pepper

1. Preheat the grill to high and line a baking sheet with foil. Put the chillies and green peppers, cut-side down, on the baking sheet and cook for about 10 minutes for the chillies and about 25 minutes for the green peppers, until charred and soft. Watch closely so they do not burn. Remove with tongs, transfer to a bowl and cover with a tea towel.

2. When cool enough to handle, rub off the skins, then finely chop the flesh.

3. Transfer to a small food processor or blender with the remaining ingredients and season to taste with salt and pepper. Blend until smooth.

4. Strain the sauce through a fine sieve. The sauce can be used immediately, but is best if left to mature in an airtight container in the refrigerator for at least 2 days before using. It will keep in the refrigerator for up to 2 weeks. For guidelines on longer storage, see page 10.

GROW YOUR OWN!

So we know you love the taste of chillies ... but did you realize they're actually easy to grow yourself? You don't need to be living in a hot country or near the Equator. With a little bit of care, anyone can nurture a crop!

And the best news? You don't need a garden – chillies are best grown in pots so any little amount of outdoor space should suffice ... even a windowsill!

1. Plant in January to harvest in July – but start them off indoors. In the UK it's too cold outside for your little chilli plants until at least mid-May.

2. Fill a seed tray with compost, lightly water and place a seed in each cell or compartment of the tray. Put a bit more compost on top. Water again, cover with clingfilm and place somewhere warm (such as an airing cupboard).

3. After about a month you should see some sprouts. Remove clingfilm and move to a warm windowsill. Keep moist.

4. When your seedlings sprout a second set of leaves, carefully transplant them to small pots – and encourage growth with a weekly tomato feed.

5. At about 13 cm/5 inches tall, transplant again to bigger pots (or fit up to three in a really big pot). Support drooping plants by tying to a cane.

6. Try not to let your plants grow much above a foot tall – pinch the tops above the leaves to encourage bushiness and more flowers. Each flower should become a chilli!

7. Snip off (and eat!) the first crop while they're still green, to encourage regrowth ... and you should be harvesting chillies all the way from July to October.

THE ULTIMATE HOT-AS-HELL CHILLI SAUCE

Are you brave enough to try this? The naga chilli – also known as the ghost chilli and Bhut Jolokia – once reigned supreme as the world's hottest chilli. Turn the extractor to high before boiling the sauce and be sure to wear rubber gloves when handling!

MAKES: ABOUT 175 ML/ 6 FL OZ

PREP TIME: 15 MINS PLUS STANDING

COOK TIME: 15 MINS

INGREDIENTS

1 tbsp allspice berries, lightly crushed

1 tbsp coriander seeds, toasted and lightly crushed

2 tsp cumin seeds, toasted

1 tsp fennel seeds, toasted

8 dried naga chillies

2 dried habanero chillies

1 carrot, about 100 g/3½ oz, thinly sliced

1 celery stick, chopped

1 small red onion, chopped

350 ml/12 fl oz cider vinegar

125 ml/4 fl oz water, plus extra if needed

4 tbsp soft light brown sugar

2 red chargrilled peppers from a jar, chopped

1. Turn the extractor to high or open a window to allow air to circulate. Place the berries and seeds in a square of muslin, gather together the sides and tie into a bag, then place in a saucepan. Stir in all the chillies, the carrot, celery, onion, vinegar and water, adding extra water to cover all the ingredients. Weigh down the chillies with a small plate.

2. Bring to the boil and boil for 5 minutes. Remove from the heat, stir in the sugar and leave to stand, covered, for at least 1 hour. Press the bag firmly with a spoon to extract as much flavour as possible.

3. Remove and discard the muslin bag. Strain the remaining contents of the pan, then remove the chilli stems. Transfer the chillies to a food processor with the red peppers, carrot, celery and onion.

4. Purée and add 1–2 tablespoons of the cooking liquid. Pass the sauce through a sieve, rubbing backwards and forwards with a spoon and scraping the sieve to produce as much purée as possible.

5. Allow to cool then leave to mature for 2 weeks in an airtight container in the refrigerator. It will keep for 1 month in the refrigerator. For guidelines on longer storage, see page 10.

SAUCY RECIPES!

TEXAS-STYLE CHILLI

Texans don't tolerate beans or any other additions in their big bowls of chilli. What you see is what you get – just chunks of beef and hot chilli sauce. It's plain and simple, and utterly delicious.

SERVES: 4   **PREP TIME: 10 MINS**   **COOK TIME: 3 HRS**

INGREDIENTS

2 tbsp rendered bacon fat, sunflower oil or rapeseed oil, plus extra, if needed

750 g/1 lb 10 oz stewing steak, cut into 2.5-cm/1-inch cubes

1 large onion, finely chopped

1 large garlic clove, finely chopped

1 tbsp dried red chilli flakes

1 serving Texan Chilli Sauce (see page 54)

1 tbsp masa harissa

1 tbsp red wine vinegar

salt and pepper

cooked rice and soured cream, to serve

1. Heat the fat in a large, heavy-based saucepan over a medium heat. Season the beef to taste with salt and pepper. Working in batches, add the beef to the pan and fry, stirring occasionally, until brown on all sides, adding extra fat as needed. Set aside the beef and juices.

2. Pour off all but 1 tablespoon of the fat. Add the onion to the pan and fry for 3–5 minutes, or until soft. Add the garlic and chilli flakes and fry for a further minute. Return the beef and all the juices to the pan and stir in the Texan Sauce. Cover and bring to the boil, then reduce the heat to low and simmer for 2¼–2½ hours, until the beef is tender.

3. Put the harissa into a small bowl and stir in the vinegar. Stir the mixture into the chilli and simmer for 10 minutes, or until the chilli thickens. Season to taste. Serve in bowls over rice, with soured cream.

HERO TIPS

All that's required to make this chilli into an evening meal is some cooked rice or tortilla crisps on the side!

PULLED PORK BURRITOS

This is a recipe that takes its time to cook, but the end result is so delicious that it's worth it! A gentle, pleasing aroma of the chipotle chillies in the sauce fills the kitchen while the pork roasts slowly.

SERVES: 4　　　**PREP TIME: 10 MINS**　　　**COOK TIME: 6 HRS**

INGREDIENTS

800 g/1 lb 12 oz boneless pork shoulder

4 tbsp passata

1 serving Chipotle & Lime Inferno Sauce (see page 48)

2 tbsp chopped fresh coriander

freshly squeezed lime juice, to taste (optional)

salt and pepper

TO SERVE

shredded cos lettuce

8 soft flour tortillas

warmed guacamole (optional)

chopped spring onions (optional)

chopped pickled jalapeños (optional)

Louisiana Hot Pepper Sauce (see page 80)

1. Preheat the oven to 220°C/425°F/Gas Mark 7. Take a piece of foil large enough to enclose the pork and use to line a baking tray, shiny-side up.

2. Season the pork to taste with salt and pepper and place in the middle of the foil. Pour over the passata and half of the Chipotle & Lime Inferno Sauce. Wrap the foil around the meat and secure the seams. Roast in the preheated oven for 30 minutes.

3. Reduce the oven temperature to 120°C/250°F/Gas Mark ½. Roast for a further 5 hours, or until the meat is very soft when you squeeze the foil packet. Remove from the oven and leave to rest, wrapped, for 20 minutes.

4. Heat the remaining sauce in a saucepan and add the cooking juices from the pork packet. Discard the pork rind and fat. Use two forks to shred the meat, then stir into the sauce. Add the coriander, and the lime juice, if using. Adjust the seasoning, if necessary.

5. Place the shredded lettuce in the centre of a tortilla, then add the pork mixture and chosen toppings. Top with the hot sauce and fold up the tortilla. Repeat with the other tortillas, then serve.

BLAZING HOT WINGS

Chicken wings are famous for being quick, easy and finger-lickingly tasty – and this recipe ticks all three boxes. To prepare ahead, coat the wings with the sticky marinade up to a day in advance.

SERVES: 4   **PREP TIME: 10 MINS**   **COOK TIME: 30-35 MINS**
                       PLUS MARINATING

INGREDIENTS

4 tbsp maple syrup

1 tbsp Louisiana Hot Pepper Sauce (page 80)

24 chicken wings, wingtips removed and each wing cut into 2 pieces at the 'elbow' joint

sunflower oil, for brushing

salt and pepper

BLUE CHEESE DRESSING

125 g/4½ oz blue cheese

1 tbsp English mustard

300 ml/10 fl oz soured cream

2 tbsp finely snipped chives

salt and pepper

1. Combine the maple syrup and Louisiana Hot Pepper Sauce in a large bowl. Season to taste with salt and pepper.

2. Add the chicken wings and rub in the sauce mixture. Set aside at room temperature for 30 minutes. If making in advance, cover the bowl with clingfilm and chill in the refrigerator until 30 minutes before cooking.

3. When ready to grill, preheat the grill to high. Line the grill tray with foil, shiny-side up, and brush the rack with oil.

4. Arrange the chicken wing pieces on the rack, fleshy-side down. Position the rack 13 cm/5 inches from the heat and cook for 20 minutes, basting occasionally with any marinade left in the bowl.

5. Turn the chicken pieces over, baste and continue to cook for 10–15 minutes, or until the skin is dark golden brown and the juices run clear when the thickest part of the meat is pierced with a sharp knife.

6. Meanwhile, to make the dressing, blend the cheese, mustard and soured cream in a small food processor or blender. Stir in the chives and season to taste with salt and pepper. Cover and chill until required.

7. Serve the chicken wings hot, at room temperature or chilled, with the dressing on the side.

A WORLD OF FLAVOUR

Although chillies originated in South and Central America, they are now grown in just about every part of the world – and have contributed to the many sauce flavours we now associate with particular regions.

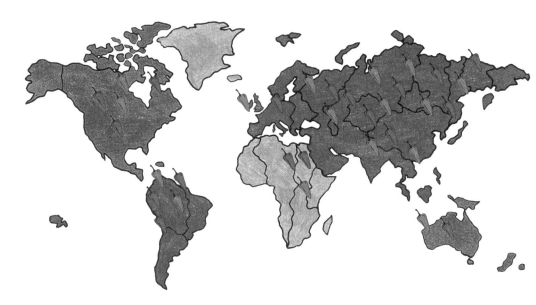

SOUTH AMERICA

The home of the chilli produces a traditionally mild cuisine – so the addition of a sauce is often needed to add a little fire. The most popular remains Adobo sauce, made from chillies, such as chipotle, with Mexican oregano, onions and tomatoes; but almost every amateur chef will have his own recipe, often using chipotle or jalapeño chillies.

USA

Known locally simply as hot sauces, US flavours are made with chillies, vinegar and salt – but often with the addition of fruits and vegetables as diverse as raspberries, mangoes, tomatoes and carrots to mellow out the flavour or add a thick edge to the sauce. The most popular chillies used in US sauces are jalapeño, chipotle, habanero and cayenne, and the results range from very mild barbecue sauces to the spicy hot pepper sauce – which can even be aged in wooden casks, like wine.

CARIBBEAN

Sauces made from chillies feature heavily in Caribbean cuisine and, like their US cousins, most are made with the addition of fruit and vegetables to temper the flavour. However, as most Caribbean sauces feature habanero and Scotch bonnet chillies, the results still tend to be far hotter! Home-made sauces are very common too, with flavours as strong as onions and garlic often added for extra piquancy.

EUROPE

Believe it or not, two of the hottest chilli sauces in the world originate from the UK! Made from the Naga Viper and Infinity chillies, they remain a specialized taste for most. However, the Portuguese peri-peri sauce, made from crushed peri-peri chillies with lime, citrus peel, garlic and various herbs, remains popular across the continent.

MIDDLE EAST

The ancients of this region believed that chillies held near-magical healing powers, and so much of the traditional cuisine features sauces with chillies as ingredients. The most popular remains harissa – made from fresh and dried hot chillies and seasoned with caraway seeds.

ASIA

As you might expect, chilli sauces are very popular in Asia and used to flavour almost all of their native cuisine. Often made with the addition of beans, much Asian chilli sauce is made as a thick paste, which can be added to curries, as a dipping sauce or for stir-frying.

JERK CHICKEN

Authentic Jamaican jerk chicken has a unique flavour from being very slowly cooked over pimento, or allspice, wood. You might not be able to replicate the exact flavour at home, but this recipe gives you the heat of true Jamaican jerk.

SERVES: 4

PREP TIME: 10 MINS PLUS MARINATING

COOK TIME: 40 MINS

INGREDIENTS

4 chicken legs

1 serving of Jamaican Jerk Sizzling Sauce (see page 78)

sunflower oil, for brushing

coleslaw, pineapple and rice salad, to serve (optional)

1. Use a fork to pierce the chicken legs all over. Place the chicken in a bowl in a single layer. Pour over the Jamaican Jerk Sizzling Sauce and rub into the chicken pieces. Cover the bowl with clingfilm and marinate in the refrigerator for at least 4 hours, or for up to 36 hours.

2. Remove the chicken from the refrigerator 30 minutes in advance of cooking. Light a barbecue and heat until the coals turn grey. Alternatively, preheat the grill to high and oil the grill rack.

3. Place the chicken pieces on the rack, fleshy-side down. Brush with some of the sauce remaining in the bowl and cook for 20 minutes.

4. Turn the chicken over and cook for a further 20 minutes, brushing with the remaining sauce, or until it is cooked through and the juices run clear when the thickest part of the flesh is pierced with a sharp knife.

5. Transfer the chicken to a warmed plate and leave to rest for 5 minutes. Use a cleaver to cut each leg into 4 pieces, then serve with coleslaw, pineapple and rice salad, if using.

TURKEY MOLE

This is a great dish for entertaining as the sauce can be made up to 5 days in advance. One word of caution, however – do not leave the simmering sauce unattended for long, as it will stick to the base of the pan.

SERVES: 4   **PREP TIME: 1-1¼ HRS**   **COOK TIME: 35 MINS**

INGREDIENTS

2 tbsp sunflower oil or rapeseed oil

1 red onion, finely chopped

4 garlic cloves, finely chopped

1 serving Scorching Mole Sauce (see page 70)

salt and pepper

chopped fresh coriander and toasted pumpkin seeds, to garnish

cooked rice, to serve

MEXICAN TURKEY STOCK

1.25 kg/2 lb 12 oz turkey pieces, such as legs and thighs, skinned

2 bay leaves

2 red chillies, chopped

2 onions, unpeeled and halved

several fresh coriander sprigs, tied

1 tsp black peppercorns, lightly crushed

1 tsp coriander seeds, lightly crushed

1. To make the stock, put the turkey pieces into a large saucepan with water to cover. Bring to the boil and skim the surface. When the scum stops forming, add the remaining stock ingredients and season to taste with salt. Bring the water to a boil, then reduce the heat to low, partially cover the pan and simmer for 45 minutes–1 hour, or until the turkey is cooked through. Remove the turkey and set aside.

2. When the turkey is cool, remove the meat from the bones and cut into bite-sized pieces. Set aside. Strain the stock into a bowl and set aside. Heat the oil in a large, heavy-based saucepan over a medium heat. Add the onion and fry for 3–5 minutes, or until soft. Add the garlic and fry for a further minute.

3. Add the Mole Sauce and 150 ml/5 fl oz of the stock and bring to the boil. Reduce the heat to low and stir in the turkey, until it is coated in sauce.

4. Leave the mole to simmer for 15–20 minutes, or until the sauce reduces. Adjust the seasoning, if necessary. Garnish with chopped coriander and toasted pumpkin seeds and serve with rice.

2

3

PRAWN & CHICKEN GUMBO

The Creole-style gumbo originated in Louisiana, USA, in the 18th century. Serve this recipe with a bowl of Louisiana Hot Pepper Sauce or harissa on the table for diners who just can't get enough heat!

SERVES: 4   **PREP TIME: 10 MINS**   **COOK TIME: 30 MINS**

INGREDIENTS

2 tbsp sunflower oil or corn oil

½ red onion, thinly sliced

100g/3½ oz spicy sausage, such as chorizo, skinned and chopped

400 g/14 oz skinless, boneless chicken thighs, cut into bite-sized pieces

1 serving Creole Gumbo Flamin' Sauce (see page 50)

150 ml/5 fl oz chicken stock or vegetable stock

400 g/14 oz large cooked peeled prawns

salt and pepper

chopped spring onions, to garnish

cooked rice and Louisiana Hot Pepper Sauce (see page 80) or Feel-The-Heat Harissa (see page 52), to serve

1. Heat the oil in a large saucepan over a medium–high heat. Add the onion and fry for 3–5 minutes, or until soft. Add the sausage and fry until brown all over.

2. Add the chicken pieces and fry for 1–2 minutes, or until lightly coloured.

3. Add the Creole Gumbo Sauce and stock and bring to the boil. Reduce the heat to low and simmer, uncovered, for 15–20 minutes, or until the chicken is cooked through and tender.

4. Increase the heat, add the prawns and stir for 2–3 minutes, or until the prawns are cooked through. Adjust the seasoning, if necessary.

5. To serve, put a mound of rice in the middle of four bowls and ladle the gumbo around each mound. Garnish with chopped spring onions and serve immediately, with Louisiana Hot Pepper Sauce or Feel-The-Heat Harissa on top.

MEATBALLS IN ADOBO SAUCE

When you're expecting chilli lovers for dinner, this is a great quick and easy dish to serve. The sauce is spicy hot and any leftovers make a great taco filling.

SERVES: 4   **PREP TIME: 20 MINS**   **COOK TIME: 20-25 MINS**

INGREDIENTS

40 g/1½ oz dried breadcrumbs

3–4 tbsp milk

3 tbsp plain flour, for dusting

250 g/9 oz lean beef mince

250 g/9 oz lean pork mince

4 large garlic cloves, finely chopped

2 eggs, beaten

3 tbsp finely chopped fresh parsley or coriander

1 tsp ground cinnamon

1 tsp sweet paprika

4 tbsp sunflower oil, for frying, plus extra if needed

1 serving Dangerous Adobo Sauce (see page 84)

125 g/4½ oz mozzarella cheese, roughly chopped

4 tbsp coarsely grated Cheddar cheese

salt and pepper

1. Combine the breadcrumbs and milk in a bowl and leave to soak for 10 minutes. Put the flour on a plate and set aside. Preheat the oven to 200°C/400°F/Gas Mark 6.

2. Combine the beef, pork, garlic, eggs, parsley, cinnamon and paprika with the breadcrumb mixture in a large bowl. Season to taste with salt and pepper and stir to combine.

3. Using wet hands, shape the mixture into 24 equal-sized balls. Heat the oil in a large frying pan over a medium heat. Working in batches, lightly roll the meatballs in the flour, shaking off the excess. Add the meatballs and fry, turning, until brown all over, then transfer to a baking dish.

4. Pour the Adobo Sauce over the meatballs in the dish, then sprinkle over the mozzarella cheese and Cheddar cheese. Bake in the preheated oven for 15–20 minutes, or until the meatballs are cooked through, the sauce is hot and the cheese is melting.

5. Meanwhile, preheat the grill to high. Place the dish under the grill and brown for 2–3 minutes.

GRILLED TERIYAKI SALMON

The heat of the wasabi paste in this marinade will surprise most aficionados of Japanese food and delight everyone who enjoys food that wakes up the taste buds. This simple recipe makes an elegant main course.

SERVES: 4

PREP TIME: 5 MINS PLUS MARINATING

COOK TIME: 10 MINS

INGREDIENTS

4 salmon fillets, each about 2.5 cm/1 inch thick

1 serving of Volatile Teriyaki Sauce (see page 72)

sunflower oil, for greasing and brushing

salt and pepper

toasted sesame seeds and a mixed salad, to serve

1. Put the salmon into a non-metallic bowl and rub the sauce into the fillets. Season to taste with salt and pepper. Leave to marinate for at least 1 hour, or for up to 3 hours, if possible.

2. Preheat the grill to high. Grease the rack with the oil and position the rack about 10 cm/4 inches from the heat.

3. Put the fillets on the rack, skin-side up, brush with any marinade remaining in the bowl and cook for 4 minutes.

4. Gently turn the fillets over, brush again with any remaining marinade and cook for a further 4–6 minutes, or until the salmon is cooked through and flakes easily.

5. Leave to rest for a few minutes, then sprinkle with the sesame seeds and serve with the mixed salad.

HERO TIPS

Any leftover sauce can be heated and drizzled over the cooked salmon. If the sauce is too thick, thin it with a little sake.

PERI-PERI CHICKEN

Peri-peri restaurants have red-hot charcoal grills that give a crisp finish to the chicken skin. This recipe gives a lightly charred skin with all the flavour of the restaurant version.

SERVES: 4-6

PREP TIME: 20 MINS PLUS MARINATING

COOK TIME: 40 MINS

INGREDIENTS

1 litre/1¾ pints water, plus extra, if needed

1 tbsp sea salt

2 bay leaves

2 garlic cloves, chopped

1 red or green jalapeño chilli, thinly sliced

1 small bunch fresh thyme

1 chicken, about 1.6 kg/ 3 lb 8 oz, spatchcocked

sunflower oil, for greasing

1 serving Peri-Peri At Your Peril Sauce (see page 76)

salt and pepper

1. Put the water into a large, non-metallic bowl with the salt, bay leaves, garlic, chilli and thyme. Submerge the chicken in the water, pushing the flavourings underneath. Cover with clingfilm and marinate in the refrigerator for 8–24 hours.

2. Remove the chicken from the liquid 30 minutes before you want to cook it, then rinse under cold running water and dry completely. Set aside.

3. Meanwhile, preheat the grill to high. Line the grill tray with foil, brush the rack with oil and position it 13 cm/5 inches from the heat.

4. When ready to cook, rub half the Peri-Peri At Your Peril Sauce onto both sides of the chicken. Place the chicken on the rack, breast-side down, and cook for 20 minutes, brushing once with some of the remaining sauce.

5. Turn the chicken over, brush with more sauce and cook for a further 15–20 minutes, basting once or twice, until the skin is lightly charred and the juices run clear when the thickest part of the meat is pierced with a sharp knife. Leave to rest for 5 minutes, then sprinkle with salt and pepper, cut into individual portions and serve.

RED-HOT BEEF FAJITAS

These Tex-Mex fajitas get a new lease of life with fresh Red-Hot Green Sauce. This is a great dish for entertaining, since both the marinated beef and the sauce can be prepared ahead. What could be easier?

SERVES: 4

PREP TIME: 15 MINS PLUS MARINATING

COOK TIME: 10-15 MINS

INGREDIENTS

4 large garlic cloves, roughly chopped

1 tsp ancho chilli powder or other chilli powder

450 g/1 lb flank steak, in one piece

4 tbsp freshly squeezed lime juice

2 tbsp sunflower oil

1 large red onion, thinly sliced

2 green peppers, deseeded and thinly sliced

2 red peppers, deseeded and thinly sliced

salt and pepper

TO SERVE

shredded cos lettuce

8 soft flour tortillas, warmed

Red-Hot Green Sauce, to taste (see page 58)

soured cream (optional)

grated Cheddar cheese or Red Leicester cheese (optional)

1. Crush the garlic and chilli powder into a paste using a pestle and mortar.

2. Put the steak into a non-metallic bowl and rub both sides with the lime juice, then rub in the garlic paste. Cover and marinate in the refrigerator for at least 8 hours, ideally for 24 hours, rubbing the marinade into the meat once or twice. Remove from the refrigerator 30 minutes before cooking.

3. Heat the oil in a frying pan. Add the onion and fry for 3 minutes. Add the green and red peppers, season to taste with salt and pepper and fry for a further 3–5 minutes, or until soft. Set aside and keep warm.

4. Meanwhile, heat a ridged, cast-iron pan over a very high heat. Add the beef and cook for 3 minutes on each side for medium–rare. Leave to rest for 5 minutes, then cut into thin slices across the grain.

5. To assemble each fajita, place a row of shredded lettuce in the centre of a tortilla, then top with the pepper and onion mixture, beef slices and Red-Hot Green Sauce. Add soured cream and grated cheese, if using. Fold up the bottom of the tortilla, then fold over the sides, burrito style, and serve immediately.

INDEX